Arduino 101: A Beginner's Guide to Arduino Design and Programming.

Table of Contents

Dedication

This work is dedicated to the passionate tinkerers, the Hecanets around the world, the 9J enthusiasts, and all those who embrace innovation and technology with love and curiosity.

May your tinkering spirit continue to inspire and drive the world forward.

Acknowledgement

We extend our heartfelt gratitude to the entire members HecaWorld unLTD for their unwavering love and dedication. Your tireless efforts and sacrifices have made this project a reality, and we are profoundly grateful for your contributions.

We would also like to express our deep appreciation to the vibrant Arduino community. Your ideas, support, and collaboration have been instrumental in shaping and enriching this work.

Furthermore, we would like to acknowledge the invaluable contributions of various AI tools used for content generation, editing, and publishing. Their capabilities have played a significant role in bringing this project to fruition. We extend our sincere thanks for their valuable assistance.

Together, with the collective efforts of passionate individuals, supportive communities, and innovative technologies, we celebrate the spirit of collaboration and creativity that has made this work possible.

Introduction

What is Arduino?

Arduino is a popular open-source platform used to create electronic projects. It consists of a programmable microcontroller board and a development environment that simplifies the process of writing code and uploading it to the board.

The platform was created in Italy in 2003 by students aiming to provide an affordable tool for non-engineers in creating interactive projects. Initially called 'Wiring', it evolved in 2005 with added support for cheaper microcontrollers.

The resulting project, a fork from Wiring, is now known as Arduino. Since then, Arduino has become a staple in the DIY electronics community, enabling hobbyists and professionals alike to build everything from robots and drones to home automation systems and musical instruments.

One of the reasons why Arduino has gained such popularity is its ease of use. The development environment, which can be downloaded for free from the Arduino website, offers a simple interface for writing code and uploading it to the board. Even those with no programming experience can learn how to use it in a matter of hours.

Another advantage of Arduino is its flexibility. The platform can be used with a wide range of sensors, actuators, and other components, making it possible to create projects that interact with the physical world in countless ways. Additionally, there are many third-party libraries available that make it easy to interface with these components, saving time and effort in the development process.

Finally, Arduino is open source, meaning that the hardware and software designs are freely available for anyone to use, modify, and distribute. This has led to a large and active community of users who share their projects, knowledge, and resources online, making it easy for newcomers to jump in and start creating.

In summary, Arduino is an accessible, flexible, and open-source platform for building electronic projects. Whether you are a beginner or an experienced electronics enthusiast, it is a great tool to have in your toolkit.

Why Learn Arduino?

Arduino is an open-source electronics platform that allows you to create interactive projects by using a microcontroller and various sensors and actuators. It is a versatile tool that can be used to automate your home, build robots, create wearable technology, and much more. In this section, we will explore why learning Arduino is essential for electronics enthusiasts and do-it- yourselfers.

1.Easy to Use

One of the main advantages of Arduino is its simplicity. It is designed for beginners, and you do not need to have any prior programming experience to use it. The programming language used in Arduino is similar to C++, and there are plenty of online resources and tutorials available to help you learn it (you will find some Arduino tutorials on our YouTube channel youtube.com/hecanet). With Arduino, you can start building projects right away, making it an excellent tool for rapid prototyping.

2. Affordable

Arduino is an affordable platform that is accessible to everyone. The cost of an Arduino board is relatively low compared to other microcontrollers on the market. You can purchase an Arduino board for as little as $15.00 or less (depending on the marketplace and the Arduino version chosen), making it an excellent choice for beginners who want to experiment with electronics without breaking the bank.

3. Customizable

Arduino is highly customizable, and you can modify it to suit your specific needs. You can add sensors like temperature sensor, humidity sensor, light sensor, Infrared sensors, pressure sensors etc., and actuators like LEDs, motors, and other components to your Arduino board to create unique projects. The platform is also open source, which means that you can modify the code and share your projects with others.

4. In-demand Skill

Arduino is a popular platform, and the demand for electronics enthusiasts who can use it is increasing. Learning Arduino can open up a world of opportunities for you, from creating your own startup to working as a freelance electronics engineer. It is also an excellent addition to your resume if you are looking for a job in the electronics industry.

In conclusion, learning Arduino is crucial for those who have an interest in electronics and enjoy DIY projects. Arduino is designed to be easy to use, affordable, and can be customized according to your needs.

Moreover, it is a highly sought-after skill in various fields. By exploring Arduino, you unlock a realm of endless possibilities that allow your creativity to soar. With Arduino, you can bring your ideas to life and develop projects that have the potential to make a positive impact on the world.

What You Need to Get Started

When you first decide to dive into the world of Arduino, it can be overwhelming to figure out where to start. However, with a few key components and some basic knowledge, you can easily get started on your first project.

Here are the essential items you may need to get started with Arduino:

1.**An Arduino board:** This is the heart of your project and the device that you will program to carry out specific tasks. There are several types of Arduino boards available, but most beginners start with the Arduino Uno, which is the most popular and versatile board.

2. **A USB cable:** You will need a USB cable to connect your Arduino board to your computer. Make sure you have a cable that is compatible with your specific board. Most Arduino boards come with a compatible USB cable as a bundle.

3. **Breadboard:** A breadboard is a device used to prototype electronic circuits. It allows you to connect components quickly and easily without the need for soldering.

4. **Jumper wires:** You will need jumper wires to connect your components to your breadboard. These wires come in assorted sizes, colors, and connection types (male to male, male to female, female to female), so make sure you have a variety on hand.

5. **Resistors:** Resistors are used to limit the flow of electricity in a circuit. You will need resistors of different values to control the amount of current in your project. 100, 220, 1k, 2k2, 10k, 1M, 10M Ohms are some of the more common values used.

6. **LEDs:** LEDs are light-emitting diodes that can be used to indicate the status of your project. They come in assorted colors

and sizes, so choose the ones that best fit your needs.

7.**Sensors:** Sensors are devices that detect changes in the environment and send signals to your Arduino board. There are many types of sensors available, including temperature sensors, humidity sensors, and motion sensors.

8.**Servo motors:** Servo motors are small motors that can be used to control the movement of objects in your project. They are commonly used in robotics projects.

With these components in hand, you can start exploring the world of Arduino and experimenting with your own projects. Remember that Arduino is a platform that allows you to combine hardware and software in creative ways, so do not be afraid to think 'outside the box' and try new things.

It is worth considering that while these components are crucial to begin with, you might also find it helpful to simulate your project online before proceeding.

You can visit https://www.circuito.io/ and access the simulation tool by clicking on the **"GO TO APP"** button.

Happy tinkering!

Hardware

Hardware is a crucial component of any electronic project, and Arduino is no exception. In this section, we will discuss the various hardware components that make up an Arduino board and how they interact with each other.

The Arduino board itself is made up of several key components, including a microcontroller, voltage regulator, and input/output pins. The microcontroller is the brain of the board, responsible for processing data and executing instructions. The voltage regulator ensures that the board receives a steady supply of power, while the input/output pins allow for communication with other devices.

One of the primary advantages of Arduino is its versatility. The board can be expanded and customized with a wide range of add-on components, including sensors, motors, and displays. These components can be connected to the board via the input/output pins, allowing for a wide range of applications.

When working with Arduino, it is essential to understand the role of the various hardware components and how they interact with each other. For example, the voltage regulator ensures that the board receives a stable supply of power, which is crucial for reliable operation. Likewise, the input/output pins are essential for sending and receiving data from other devices, such as sensors or displays.

Another important consideration when working with Arduino hardware is compatibility. There are many types of Arduino boards available, each with its own unique features and compatibility requirements. It is essential to choose the right board for your project and ensure that any additional components are compatible with the board you are using.

In conclusion, hardware is a critical component of any electronic project, including Arduino. Understanding the various hardware components and how they interact with each other is essential for successful Arduino projects. With the right hardware and a basic understanding of how it works, the possibilities for Arduino projects are endless.

Software

Software is a crucial aspect of Arduino projects. It is the driving force that makes your project come to life. Without software, your Arduino board would be nothing more than a simple circuit board. In this subchapter, we will discuss the several types of software that are used in Arduino projects.

The Arduino Integrated Development Environment (IDE) is the

primary software used in Arduino projects. It is an open-source software that is free to download and use. The IDE is a code editor that allows you to write and upload code to your Arduino board. It supports multiple programming languages, including C and C++. The IDE also comes with a library of pre-written code, called sketches, that you can use in your projects.

Another important software used in Arduino projects is the firmware. Firmware is a type of software that is built into the hardware of the Arduino board. It controls the functions of the board and allows it to communicate with other devices. The firmware for Arduino boards is pre-installed and can be updated as needed.

There are also many third-party software applications that can be used with Arduino boards. For example, Processing is a software application that is often used with Arduino projects. Processing is a programming language and environment that is used to create interactive graphics and animations. It can be used to create programs that communicate with Arduino boards and control their functions.

In addition to software, there are also many online resources available to help you with your Arduino projects. There are online forums and communities where you can ask questions and get help from other Arduino enthusiasts. There are also many websites that offer tutorials and project ideas.

In conclusion, software is an essential component of Arduino projects. The Arduino IDE, firmware, and third-party software applications are all important tools that are used in Arduino projects. With the right software and resources, you can create amazing projects that will impress your friends and family.

How to Use This Book

Welcome to Arduino 101: A Beginner's Guide to Arduino Design and Programming. This book is designed to introduce the basics of Arduino to beginners who are interested in learning about electronics.

The book is divided into chapters, each focusing on a specific topic related to Arduino. You can read the book from start to finish or skip around to the chapters that interest you the most.

Before going any further, there are a few things you should know about how to use this book.

Firstly, this book assumes that you have a basic understanding of electronics. If you are completely new to electronics, it may be helpful to brush up on some basic concepts before diving into Arduino. You can find plenty of online resources, including other materials from HecaWorld unLTD, that can help you with this.

Secondly, this book assumes that you have access to an Arduino board. If you do not have an Arduino board, you can purchase one online or at a local electronics store. There are many different models of Arduino boards, but for the purposes of this book, we will be using the Arduino Uno.

Thirdly, this book is designed to be hands-on. Each chapter includes practical examples and projects that you can build with your Arduino board. We encourage you to follow along and build these projects yourself, as this is the best way to learn.

Finally, this book is not meant to be a comprehensive guide to Arduino. There is always more to learn, and we encourage you to explore the Arduino community and experiment with your own projects.

With these tips in mind, we hope that you find this book to be a helpful introduction to Arduino. We believe that Arduino is a powerful tool for anyone interested in electronics, and we hope that this book inspires you to explore the possibilities of this amazing platform.

Getting Started with Arduino

Setting Up the Arduino Environment

Before you can start using Arduino, you need to set up the development environment. The Arduino IDE (Integrated Development Environment) is a software that allows you to write, compile, and upload code to the Arduino board. Here are the steps to set up the Arduino environment:

1. Download and Install the Arduino IDE

The first step is to download and install the Arduino IDE on your computer. You can download the latest version of the IDE from the Arduino website. Once the download is complete, open the installer and follow the instructions to install the software.

2. Connect the Arduino Board

Once you have installed the IDE, you need to connect the Arduino board to your computer using a USB cable. The Arduino board should be detected automatically by your computer.

3. Select the Board and Port

Before you can start uploading code to the Arduino board, you need to select the board and port in the IDE. To do this, go to the Tools menu and select Board and Port. Select the board that you are using (e.g., Arduino UNO) and the port that the board is connected to.

4. Upload a Test Program

Now that you have set up the environment, it is time to test it by uploading a simple program to the Arduino board. In the IDE, go to *File > Examples > Basics > Blink*. This will open a program that blinks an LED connected to pin 13 of the Arduino board. Click on the Upload button (the right arrow icon) to upload the program to the board.

5. Verify the Program

Once the program is uploaded, you should see the LED on the board blinking. If the LED is not blinking, check your connections and try uploading the program again.

In conclusion, setting up the Arduino environment is a straightforward process that requires only a few steps. Once you have set up the environment, you can start writing and uploading your own programs to the Arduino board. With a little bit of practice, you can create all kinds of electronic projects using Arduino.

Installing the Arduino IDE

Installing the Arduino IDE is the first step towards beginning your journey into the world of electronics with Arduino. The Arduino IDE is an integrated development environment that allows you to write, compile and upload code to the Arduino board.

In this section, we will provide a step-by-step guide to help you download and install the Arduino Integrated Development Environment (IDE).

Step 1: Visit the Arduino Website
Go to the official Arduino website at www.arduino.cc.

Step 2: Navigate to the Software Page
Click on the "Software" tab or look for the "Download" section on the website's homepage.

Step 3: Choose Your Operating System
Select your operating system from the available options. Arduino IDE is compatible with Windows, macOS, and Linux.

Step 4: Download the Arduino IDE

Click on the download link provided for your operating system. The download should start automatically. If not, click on the provided download button.

Step 5: Locate the Downloaded File

Once the download is complete, locate the downloaded file on your computer. It is usually saved in the "Downloads" folder or the designated folder for downloaded files.

Step 6: Install the Arduino IDE

Double-click on the downloaded file to start the installation process. Follow the on-screen instructions to proceed with the installation. Make sure to review and accept the terms and conditions if prompted.

Step 7: Select Installation Options

During the installation, you may be presented with options to customize the installation. You can choose the desired components and features you want to include. If you are unsure, it is recommended to leave the default settings.

We recommend that you choose the default location to avoid any compatibility issues.

Step 8: Complete the Installation

Once the installation is complete, you will see a confirmation message. You can now launch the Arduino IDE from your desktop or through the Start menu.

Step 9: Connect Your Arduino Board

Before you start programming, connect your Arduino board to your computer using a USB cable. Make sure the board is properly recognized by your computer.

Step 10: Open the Arduino IDE

Launch the Arduino IDE. You will be greeted with the main interface, where you can start writing and uploading code to your Arduino board.

Congratulations! You have successfully downloaded and installed the Arduino IDE. You are now ready to begin your journey into the exciting world of Arduino programming.

After the installation is complete, you can launch the Arduino IDE and start writing code. The IDE comes with a sample program that you can use to 'test' your installation. To do this, click on *File > Examples > 01. Basics > Blink*. This will open a new window with the Blink code, which you can upload to your Arduino board.

To upload the code to the board, you need to connect your board to your computer using a USB cable. Make sure that the correct board and port are selected in the Tools menu. Then, click on the upload button, and the IDE will compile and upload the code to your board.

In conclusion, installing the Arduino IDE is an uncomplicated process that can be completed in a few minutes. Once you have installed the IDE, you can start exploring the world of electronics with Arduino. We recommend that you take some time to familiarize yourself with the IDE and the sample programs before moving on to more complex projects. Happy tinkering!

Configuring the Arduino IDE

The Arduino Integrated Development Environment (IDE) is an open-source software that enables the creation and programming of Arduino boards. It is a user-friendly interface that simplifies the process of writing, compiling, and uploading code to the board. In this subchapter, we will discuss how to configure the Arduino IDE to work with your Arduino board.

Installation

Installation of the IDE is the first step which you would have completed in the subsection above. There are also other online simulators you could use. See example at the 'Online Simulator' subsection' below.

Board Selection

After installing the IDE, you need to select the board you want to work with. To do this, click on the "Tools" menu and select "Board." From the drop-down menu, select the Arduino board you are using. If you are working with a custom board, you can select the "Arduino/Genuino UNO" board as it is compatible with most Arduino boards.

Port Selection

The next step is to select the port your Arduino board is connected to. To do this, click on the "Tools" menu and select "Port." From the drop-down menu, select the port that your board is connected to. If you are unsure which port to select, disconnect your board and check the available ports. Reconnect your board and select the newly available port.

Sketches

A sketch is a program written in the Arduino IDE that is uploaded to the board. To create a new sketch, click on "File" and select "New." This will open a new window where you can write your code. You can also open existing sketches by clicking on "File" and selecting "Open."

Compiling and Uploading

After writing your code, you need to compile and upload it to the board. To compile the code, click on the "Verify" button. If the code contains errors, the IDE will highlight them. Once the code is error-free, click on the "Upload" button. The IDE will compile the code and upload it to the board.

Conclusion

Configuring the Arduino IDE is essential to get started with Arduino programming. By following the steps outlined in this section, you can set up the IDE to work with your Arduino board, create and upload sketches, and start working on your projects. With practice and experimentation, you can unleash the full potential of Arduino and take your electronics skills to the next level.

Online Simulation

If you choose to use an online simulator, the Arduino online simulator can be found at the following website:

Website: https://www.tinkercad.com/

Tinkercad is an online platform that offers a variety of tools for designing, simulating, and programming projects, including an Arduino simulator. It provides a virtual environment where you can build circuits, test code, and simulate the behavior of Arduino projects without the need for physical components.

To access the Arduino simulator on Tinkercad, you can follow these steps:

Step 1: Visit the Tinkercad Website
Go to the Tinkercad website at https://www.tinkercad.com/.

Step 2: Sign In or Create an Account
If you already have a Tinkercad account, sign in using your credentials. Otherwise, create a new account by clicking on the "Join Now" or "Sign Up" button.

Step 3: Access the Circuits Section
Once you are signed in, you will be taken to the Tinkercad dashboard. Click on the "Create New Design" button to start a new project. On the next screen, select the "Circuits" option to access the circuit design section.

Step 4: Start Simulating Arduino Projects
In the circuit design section, you will find a wide range of electronic components, including Arduino boards, sensors, actuators, and more. You can drag and drop these components onto the virtual breadboard and connect them to build your circuit.
To program your Arduino simulation, click on the Arduino board and open the code editor. You can write your code in the Arduino programming language (based on C/C++) and upload it to the virtual Arduino board.

Step 5: Simulate and Test Your Projects
Once your circuit is built and the code is uploaded, you can run the simulation to see how your project behaves. The virtual environment allows you to test the functionality of your Arduino projects without the need for physical components.

Tinkercad's Arduino simulator provides a convenient and user-friendly way to learn and experiment with Arduino programming and circuit design. It is a great resource for beginners and experienced users alike.

Note: Tinkercad is a web-based platform, so you will need a stable internet connection to access and use the Arduino simulator. If stable internet connection would be an issue, consider downloading and installing the IDE whenever you have a good connection and using that for your projects.

Please note that the mentioned links were active at the time of publication.

Writing Your First Program

Congratulations! You have just taken your first step into the world of programming with Arduino. Now, it is time to write your first program. Do not worry if you do not have any prior experience in programming. Arduino makes it easy for anyone to get started with programming and electronics.

To write your first program, you will need to download the Arduino software from the official website. The software is available for Windows, Mac, and Linux operating systems. Once you have installed the software, connect your Arduino board to your computer using a USB cable.

Open the Arduino software and create a new sketch by clicking on *File > New*. A new window will open where you can start writing your program. The programming language used by Arduino is based on C++ and is easy to learn. In fact, the Arduino software comes with a lot of pre-written code, or sketches, that you can use to get started.

Let us start with a simple program that turns on an LED connected to pin 13 of the Arduino board. Here is the code:

```
*********************************
// Setup function runs once at the beginning
void setup() {
   pinMode(13, OUTPUT); // Set pin 13 as OUTPUT
}

// Loop function runs repeatedly
void loop() {
   digitalWrite(13, HIGH); // Turn on the LED on pin 13
   delay(1000); // Wait for 1 second
   digitalWrite(13, LOW); // Turn off the LED on pin 13
   delay(1000); // Wait for 1 second
}
*********************************
```

In the above code, the **setup()** function is used to initialize the program. In this case, it sets pin 13 as an output pin using the **pinMode()** function.

The **loop()** function is the main part of the program that runs repeatedly. Inside the loop, the LED connected to pin 13 is turned on using **digitalWrite()** with the **HIGH** value, and then a delay of 1 second is added using **delay()**. After that, the LED is turned off using **digitalWrite()** with the **LOW** value, and another 1 second delay is added.

This creates a blinking effect where the LED turns on for 1 second and then turns off for 1 second, repeating continuously.

To upload the program to your Arduino board, click on the Upload button in the Arduino software. The software will compile your code and upload it to the board. Once the upload is complete, you will see the LED connected to pin 13 turn on and off every second.

Congratulations! You have just written your first program with Arduino. From here on, you can experiment with different sensors and actuators and write more complex programs to control them. The possibilities are endless, and with Arduino, you are only limited by your imagination.

Blinking an LED

Blinking an LED is the "Hello World" of Arduino programming. It is a simple and fun project that can be easily accomplished even by beginners. In this subchapter, we will show you how to blink an LED using an Arduino board.

First, you will need to gather the materials needed for this project. You will need an Arduino board, an LED, a resistor, and a breadboard. The LED and resistor are used to limit the current that flows through the LED.

To start, you will need to connect the LED to the Arduino

board. The LED has two pins, the longer one is the positive or anode pin, and the shorter one is the negative or cathode pin. Insert the anode pin of the LED into the breadboard and connect it to the Arduino board's digital pin 13. Next, insert the resistor's one end into the same row as the LED's cathode pin, and the other end to the ground pin on the Arduino board.

Now that you have connected the LED and resistor to the Arduino board, you can start coding. Open the Arduino IDE software and create a new sketch. In the setup function, set the digital pin 13 as an output pin by writing "pinMode(13, OUTPUT);" In the loop function, you will use the "digitalWrite" function to turn the LED on and off.

To blink the LED, write "digitalWrite(13, HIGH);" to turn the LED on, wait for a second by writing "delay(1000);" then write "digitalWrite(13, LOW);" to turn the LED off. Wait again for a second by writing "delay(1000);" before repeating the process.

Upload the code to the Arduino board by clicking on the upload button on the software. The LED should start blinking once the code is uploaded successfully.

In conclusion, blinking an LED is a simple but effective project that can introduce beginners to the basic concepts of programming and electronics using Arduino. It is an excellent starting point for more complex projects, and it is a fun way to experiment with different coding techniques.

Understanding the Code

One of the most important aspects of working with Arduino is understanding the code that runs on it. The code is what tells the Arduino what to do, and without it, the board would be nothing more than a paperweight. In this section, we will take a look at what code is, how it works, and how to write and upload it to the Arduino board.

What is Code?

At its simplest, code is a set of instructions that tell a computer what to do. In the case of Arduino, the code is written in the Arduino Integrated Development Environment (IDE) and tells the board what to do with its various inputs and outputs. The code is written in a programming language called C++, which is a powerful and versatile language used in a wide range of applications.

How Does Code Work?

When you write code for Arduino, you are essentially telling the board what to do with its various inputs and outputs. For example, you might write code that tells the board to read a sensor and turn on a light if the sensor detects a certain level of light. The board will execute the code in order, line by line, and follow the instructions you have given it.

Writing and Uploading Code to the Arduino

To write and upload code to the Arduino, you will need to use the Arduino IDE. The IDE is a software program that allows you to write, compile, and upload code to the board. When you are ready to upload your code, simply connect the board to your computer via USB and click the Upload button in the IDE. The code will be compiled and uploaded to the board, and you will be able to see the results of your code on the board's various inputs and outputs.

In Conclusion

Understanding the code is a crucial part of working with Arduino. By learning how to write and upload code, you will be able to take full advantage of the board's capabilities and create a wide range of projects. With a little bit of practice and patience, you will be well on your way to becoming an Arduino master.

Uploading Your Program to the Arduino Board

After designing and writing your program, the next step is to upload it to the Arduino board. This is a straightforward process that requires a few tools and some basic knowledge. In this subchapter, we will guide you on how to upload your program to the Arduino board.

The first step is to connect your Arduino board to your computer using a USB cable. Make sure that the USB cable is properly connected to both the computer and the Arduino board. Once the connection is established, the Arduino board's LED light will turn on, indicating that it is ready to receive data.

Next, you need to open the Arduino IDE software on your computer. This software is available for free on the Arduino website. After opening the software, select the correct board and port from the "Tools" menu. The board and port settings will depend on the type of Arduino board you are using and the USB port that you have connected it to.

Once you have selected the correct board and port, you can proceed to upload your program. To do this, click on the

"Upload" button on the Arduino IDE software. The software will compile your program and then upload it to the Arduino board. You can monitor the progress of the upload process from the status bar at the bottom of the software.

After the upload is complete, you can disconnect the USB cable from the computer and the Arduino board. Your program is now stored on the Arduino board's memory and will run whenever the board is powered on.

In conclusion, uploading your program to the Arduino board is a straightforward process that requires a few tools and some basic knowledge. By following the steps outlined in this subchapter, you can easily upload your program and start experimenting with your Arduino board. With practice, you can become proficient in programming your Arduino board and create exciting projects that highlight your creativity and skills.

Troubleshooting Common Issues

Arduino is a wonderful platform for anyone interested in electronics and programming. It offers an easy way to learn and experiment with various projects, from basic LED blinking to complex robotics. However, like any technology, it comes with its own set of challenges and issues. In this subchapter, we will discuss some of the common issues that you may encounter while working with Arduino, and how to troubleshoot them.

One of the most common issues with Arduino is connection problems. Sometimes, you may not be able to connect to your Arduino board using your computer. This may happen due to several reasons such as a faulty USB cable, a damaged USB port, or incorrect board selection. The first thing to check is if your board is properly connected to your computer, and if the USB cable is working fine. If everything seems fine, then make sure that you have selected the correct board and port in your Arduino IDE.

Another common issue is programming errors. You may encounter errors while uploading your code to the board, or your code may not work as intended. This may happen due to syntax errors, incorrect libraries, or issues with the code itself. To troubleshoot this, you can use the serial monitor to check the output of your program and debug the code line by line. You can also check if you have included all the necessary libraries and if the syntax of your code is correct.

Power issues can also cause problems while working with Arduino. Sometimes, your board may not power up at all, or it may not be able to power your peripherals. This may happen due to a faulty power source, a damaged power regulator, or incorrect wiring. To troubleshoot this, make sure that you are using the correct voltage and amperage for your board and peripherals. You can also check if your power source is working fine using a multimeter.

In conclusion, troubleshooting common issues while working with Arduino is an essential skill for any electronics enthusiast or do-it-yourselfer (DIY'er). By understanding the common issues and how to troubleshoot them, you can save time and frustration, and get back to creating amazing projects with Arduino.

Understanding Arduino Basics

Anatomy of an Arduino Board

Before delving into the world of programming an Arduino board, it is essential to understand the hardware components that make up the board. In this subchapter, we will explore the anatomy of an Arduino board and its various components.

Microcontroller

At the heart of an Arduino board lies a microcontroller unit (MCU). It is the main processing unit that controls all the functions of the board. The most commonly used microcontroller in an Arduino board is the ATmega328P, which is responsible for executing the code uploaded to it.

Power Supply

Arduino boards can be powered in diverse. The most common method is through a USB connection to a computer or a power bank. The board can also be powered through the DC jack, which takes in a voltage of 7-12V. Some boards also have a Vin pin that can accept a voltage of up to 20V.

Crystal Oscillator

The crystal oscillator is responsible for generating a stable clock signal that synchronizes the operations of the microcontroller. The Arduino board uses a 16MHz crystal oscillator.

Reset Button

The reset button is essential in resetting the board and stopping the current program execution. Pressing the button triggers the reset signal to the microcontroller, causing the code to restart execution from the beginning.

Power LED

The power LED indicates that the board is powered and receiving a voltage supply. When the LED is on, it means that the board is ready for operation.

Digital and Analog I/O Pins

Arduino boards have a series of digital and analog input/output (I/O) pins that allow for communication with external devices. Digital pins can be used as either input or output, while analog pins can measure voltage levels.

Conclusion

Understanding the anatomy of an Arduino board is crucial in developing and troubleshooting projects. By knowing the components that make up the board, you can effectively utilize its functions and capabilities.

Arduino Pinout Diagram

One of the most important aspects of working with an Arduino board is understanding the pinout diagram. The pinout diagram is essentially a map of all the pins on the board, and it helps you to identify which pins are used for which functions. This is crucial when you are programming your board, as it ensures that you are using the right pins for the right purposes in your project(s).

The Arduino board has a number of different pins, which are divided into three categories: digital pins, analog pins, and power pins. Digital pins are used for input and output, while analog pins are used for analog input. Power pins are used to power the board and any connected components.

The digital pins on the Arduino board are labeled from 0 to 13. Pin 0 and Pin 1 are used for serial communication with other devices, while Pin 2 to Pin 13 are used for general-purpose input/output (GPIO) functions. These pins can be used for a variety of purposes, such as turning on and off LEDs, reading switches, or controlling motors.

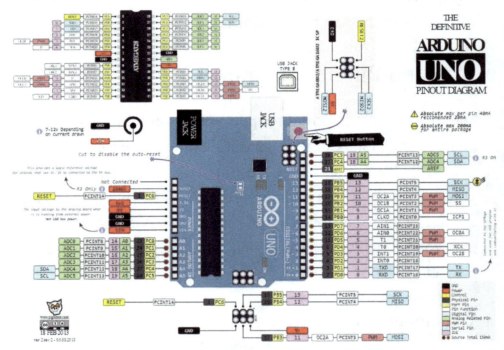

Figure 1: Pinout of ARDUINO Board and ATMega328PU
Credit: https://www.circuito.io/blog/arduino-uno-pinout/

The analog pins on the Arduino board are labeled A0 to A5. These pins are used for analog input, which means that they can read and interpret analog signals such as light, temperature, or sound. This is useful for a wide range of projects, from building a weather station to creating a musical instrument.

Finally, the power pins on the Arduino board are used to supply power to the board and any connected components. There are two main power pins: the VIN pin and the 5V pin. The VIN pin is used to supply power to the board from an external power source, such as a battery or power supply. The 5V pin is used to supply power to any connected components that require a 5V power supply.

In addition to these pins, the Arduino board also has a number of other pins that are used for specific functions, such as the reset pin, which is used to reset the board, and the ground pin, which is used to complete electrical circuits.

Overall, understanding the pinout diagram is essential for anyone working with an Arduino board. It ensures that you are using the correct pins for your project, and it helps you to avoid any potential problems or errors. By familiarizing yourself with the pinout diagram, you can confidently start exploring the world of Arduino and begin building your own electronic projects.

Digital vs Analog Signals

One of the fundamental concepts in electronics is the distinction between digital and analog signals. In this subchapter, we will explore the differences between these two types of signals and how they are used in the world of Arduino.

Digital signals are composed of discrete values, represented by binary digits (bits) that can only take on two values: 0 or 1. These signals are used to transmit information in a binary format, such as the on or off state of a switch, or the presence or absence of a pulse in a communication protocol.

Analog signals, on the other hand, are continuous signals that can take on any value within a defined range. These signals are used to represent physical quantities such as voltage, current, or temperature, and can be measured and transmitted as a continuous waveform.

In the world of Arduino, digital signals are used extensively to control and interact with the physical world. For example, a digital pin on an Arduino board can be set to either HIGH or LOW to turn an LED on or off, or to control the speed of a motor. Digital signals can also be used to communicate between different devices using protocols such as I2C, SPI, or UART.

Analog signals are also important in Arduino projects, particularly when it comes to sensing and measuring physical quantities. For example, an analog input pin on an Arduino board can be used to measure the voltage of a sensor, or the temperature of a room. These analog signals are converted into digital values using an analog-to-digital converter (ADC) built into the microcontroller, allowing them to be processed and analyzed by the Arduino program.

The choice of whether to use digital or analog signals in an Arduino project depends on the specific requirements of the project. If you need to control the on/off state of a device or transmit binary data, digital signals are the way to go. If you need to measure or sense physical quantities, analog signals are necessary.

In conclusion, understanding the differences between digital and analog signals is essential for any electronics enthusiast or DIY'er using Arduino. By using the appropriate signal type for your project, you can ensure that your Arduino project is both reliable and accurate.

Input and Output

Input and output are the two fundamental concepts that are at the heart of every Arduino project. In simple terms, input refers to any signal or data that is being sent to the Arduino, while output refers to any signal or data that is being sent out of the Arduino.

For instance, if you want to build a project that involves sensing the temperature in a room and turning on a fan when it gets too hot, you would need to connect a temperature sensor to the input pins of the Arduino. The sensor would send temperature data to the Arduino, which would then analyze the data and determine whether the fan needs to be turned on or off. The fan would be connected to the output pins of the Arduino, which would then send a signal to turn on or off the fan.

The Arduino board has multiple input and output pins that can be used to connect various sensors, actuators, and other electronic components. The input pins are labeled A0 to A5 and are used to connect analog sensors, such as light sensors, temperature sensors, and potentiometers. The output pins are labeled digital pins 0 to 13 and are used to connect various actuators, such as LEDs, motors, and relays.

To use the input and output pins of the Arduino, you need to understand the basics of programming. The Arduino programming language is based on C/C++, and you can use it to control the input and output pins of the Arduino. The programming language has various functions that allow you to read data from the input pins and send data to the output pins.

For instance, to read data from an analog sensor connected to the input pin A0, you can use the analogRead() function. This function returns a value between 0 and 1023, depending on the voltage level at the input pin. To send data to an output pin, you can use the digitalWrite() function. This function allows you to set the output pin to HIGH or LOW, depending on whether you want to turn on or off the connected component.

In conclusion, input and output are essential concepts in Arduino programming, and they play a crucial role in every electronics project. By understanding how to use the input and output pins of the Arduino, you can build various projects that involve sensing and controlling electronic components.

Understanding Variables and Data Types

In the world of programming, variables and data types are essential concepts to understand. In Arduino programming, variables are used to store data that can be accessed and manipulated throughout the program. Data types, on the other hand, define the type of data that can be stored in a variable and determine the operations that can be performed on it.

Arduino supports several data types, including integer, float, boolean, and string. Each data type has specific properties that determine how they can be used. Integers, for example, are whole numbers that can be positive or negative, while floats are numbers with decimal points. Booleans can only be either true or false, while strings are used to store text.

When declaring a variable in Arduino, the data type must be specified. For example, to declare an integer variable called "myVariable", the code would look like this:

```
int myVariable;
```

This creates a variable that can store an integer value. To assign a value to the variable, the code would look like this:

```
myVariable = 10;
```
This assigns the value of 10 to the variable "myVariable". Variables can also be declared and assigned a value in one line of code, like this:

```
int myVariable = 10;
```

In addition to data types, variables also have a scope, which determines where they can be accessed in the program. Variables declared outside of a function have global scope, meaning they can be accessed from anywhere in the program. Variables declared inside a function have local scope, meaning they can only be accessed within that function.

Understanding variables and data types is crucial for Arduino programming. With this knowledge, you can effectively store and manipulate data in your programs, making your projects more advanced and efficient. So, take the time to become familiar with these concepts, and you will be well on your way to creating amazing Arduino projects.

Using Functions and Libraries

Arduino is a powerful platform that can be used to create a variety of electronic projects. While the basic concepts of programming are relatively easy to learn, there are many advanced features that can be used to make your projects more efficient and effective. One of the most powerful features of Arduino is the ability to use functions and libraries.

Functions are blocks of code that can be reused throughout your program. They can be used to perform specific tasks, such as reading a sensor or controlling a motor. By using functions, you can simplify your code and make it easier to read and maintain. Functions can also be used to pass data between various parts of your program.

Libraries are collections of functions that are designed to perform specific tasks. There are many libraries available for Arduino, and they can be used to perform a wide range of tasks, from controlling LEDs to communicating with other devices. Libraries can be downloaded from the Arduino website or created by other users and shared online.

To use a library, you first need to install it. This can be done by downloading the library from the Arduino website and then adding it to your Arduino IDE. Once the library is installed, you can use its functions in your program by including the library in your code.

Using functions and libraries can make your Arduino projects more efficient and effective. By reusing code and taking advantage of pre-built libraries, you can save time and focus on the unique aspects of your project. Whether you are a beginner or an experienced electronics enthusiast, learning how to use functions and libraries is a crucial step in mastering the Arduino platform.

Exploring the Arduino Language

Control Structures

Control structures are fundamental programming concepts in Arduino that allow you to control the flow of execution of your program. They are essential in creating complex programs that can make decisions, repeat actions, and handle errors.

There are three main types of control structures in Arduino: decision-making structures, loop structures, and subroutines. Each of these structures has a unique purpose and syntax and understanding them is essential in creating efficient and effective programs.

Decision-Making Structures

Decision-making structures allow your program to make decisions based on certain conditions. There are two main types of decision-making structures: the if statement and the switch statement.

The if statement allows you to execute a block of code if a

certain condition is true. For example, you can use an if statement to check if a sensor has detected an object and then execute a specific action based on that.

The switch statement is similar to the if statement, but it allows you to compare a variable against multiple values and execute a block of code based on the matching value. This is useful when you have a large number of possible conditions to check.

Loop Structures

Loop structures allow you to repeat a block of code multiple times until a certain condition is met. There are two main types of loop structures: the for loop and the while loop.

The for loop is used when you know the exact number of times you want to repeat a block of code. For example, you can use a for loop to iterate through an array of values and perform a specific action on each value.

The while loop is used when you want to repeat a block of code until a certain condition is met. For example, you can use a while loop to continuously read data from a sensor until a certain threshold is reached.

Subroutines

Subroutines allow you to break your program into smaller, more manageable pieces of code. They are useful when you need to perform a specific action multiple times throughout your program.

In Arduino, subroutines are called functions. You can create your own functions or use built-in functions provided by Arduino. Functions allow you to encapsulate complex pieces of code and reuse them throughout your program.

In conclusion, control structures are essential programming concepts that allow you to create complex programs that can make decisions, repeat actions, and handle errors. Understanding how to use decision-making structures, loop structures, and subroutines is essential in creating efficient and effective programs in Arduino.

If Statements

If statements are a fundamental aspect of programming, and they play a crucial role in the functionality of Arduino projects. An if statement is a conditional statement that evaluates whether a certain condition is true or false. If the condition is true, the statements within the if block are executed. Otherwise, the statements within the else block are executed.

Here is an example:

```
*********************************
int temperature = 25; // Temperature in Centigrade/Celsius

if (temperature > 30) {
    Serial.println("It's too hot!");
} else {
    Serial.println("The temperature is just right.");
}
*********************************
```

In this example, we are using an if statement to determine whether the temperature is too hot or 'just right.' If the temperature is greater than 30, the first statement is executed, and we print "It's too hot!". Otherwise, the second statement is executed, and we print "The temperature is just right."

If statements can also be nested within each other to create more complex conditions. For example:

```
********************************
int temperature = 25;
int humidity = 60;

if (temperature > 30) {
   if (humidity > 70) {
      Serial.println("It's hot and humid!");
   } else {
      Serial.println("It's hot but not too humid.");
   }
} else {
   if (humidity > 70) {
      Serial.println("It's not too hot but it's humid.");
   } else {
      Serial.println("The temperature and humidity are just
right.");
   }
}
********************************
```

In this example, we are checking both temperature and humidity. If the temperature is greater than 30 and the humidity is greater than 70, we print "It's hot and humid!". If the temperature is greater than 30 but the humidity is less than or equal to 70, we print "It's hot but not too humid" and so on.

If statements are an essential part of Arduino programming, and they can be used in a variety of ways to create complex conditions and logic for your projects. By mastering if statements, you will have the building blocks you need to create more advanced Arduino programs.

Loops

Loops are an essential part of programming, and the Arduino is no different. In programming, a loop is a sequence of instructions that are repeated until a certain condition is met. Loops are used to automate tasks and to process data more efficiently. There are two types of loops in Arduino programming: the for loop and the while loop.

The for loop is used when you need to repeat a set of instructions a specific number of times. It consists of three parts: initialization, condition, and increment/decrement. The initialization part is executed only once, at the beginning of the loop. The condition part is evaluated before each iteration, and if it is true, the loop continues. The increment/decrement part is executed at the end of each iteration.

Here is an example of a for loop that blinks an LED 10 times:

```
**********************************
void setup() {
  pinMode(LED_BUILTIN, OUTPUT);
}
void loop() {
  for (int i = 0; i < 10; i++) {
    digitalWrite(LED_BUILTIN, HIGH);
    delay(1000);
    digitalWrite(LED_BUILTIN, LOW);
    delay(1000);
  }
}
**********************************
```

In this example, the LED_BUILTIN pin is set as an output in the setup function. Then, in the loop function, a for loop is used to blink the LED 10 times. The loop runs from i=0 to i<10, and for each iteration, the LED is turned on for one second (delay(1000)), then turned off for one second (delay(1000)).

The while loop is used when you need to repeat a set of instructions until a certain condition is met. It consists of only one part: the condition. The loop continues as long as the condition is true.

Here is an example of a while loop that reads a button and turns on an LED:

```
*********************************
const int buttonPin = 2;
const int ledPin = 13;

void setup() {
  pinMode(buttonPin, INPUT);
  pinMode(ledPin, OUTPUT);
}
void loop() {
  while (digitalRead(buttonPin) == HIGH) {
    digitalWrite(ledPin, HIGH);
  }
}
*********************************
```

In this example, the buttonPin and ledPin are defined as constants in the beginning of the sketch. In the setup function, the buttonPin is set as an input and the ledPin is set as an output. In the loop function, a while loop is used to check if the button is pressed (digitalRead(buttonPin) == HIGH). If the button is pressed, the LED is turned on (digitalWrite(ledPin, HIGH)). If the button is released, the LED is turned off (digitalWrite(ledPin, LOW)).

Loops are an important part of Arduino programming, and they allow you to automate tasks and process data more efficiently.

Whether you are using a for loop or a while loop, make sure to test your code and debug any errors before moving on to more complex projects.

Functions

Functions are one of the most important concepts in programming with Arduino. Simply put, a function is a set of instructions that performs a specific task. Functions are an essential part of Arduino programming, as they allow you to write complex programs that can be broken down into smaller, more manageable pieces.

In Arduino programming, a function is defined using the keyword "void," followed by the name of the function and a set of parentheses. For example, a simple function that turns an LED on and off might look like this:

```
**********************************
void blink_LED() {
  digitalWrite(LED_PIN, HIGH);
  delay(1000);
  digitalWrite(LED_PIN, LOW);
  delay(1000);
}
**********************************
```

In this example, the function is named "blink_LED," and it

performs two tasks: it turns the LED on, waits for a second, then turns it off and waits for another second. The LED_PIN variable is defined elsewhere in the program, and it specifies the pin that the LED is connected to.

Once you have defined a function, you can call it from anywhere in your program using its name and the parentheses. For example, you might call the "blink_LED" function from the setup() function of your program:

```
*********************************
void setup() {
  pinMode(LED_PIN, OUTPUT);
  blink_LED();
}
*********************************
```

In this example, the setup() function sets the LED_PIN to be an output pin, then calls the blink_LED function, which turns the LED on and off.

Functions can also accept arguments, which are values that are passed into the function when it is called. For example, you might write a function that takes two integers and adds them together:

```
**********************************
int add_numbers(int a, int b) {
    return a + b;
}
**********************************
```

In this example, the function is named "add_numbers," and it takes two integer arguments, "a" and "b." The function returns the sum of the two arguments.

Functions are a powerful tool in Arduino programming, and they allow you to write complex programs that are easy to read and maintain. By breaking your program down into smaller pieces, you can make it easier to debug and modify, and you can reuse code across multiple projects. If you are new to Arduino programming, functions are an essential concept to understand, and they will be an important part of your programming toolbox.

Built-in Functions

One of the most powerful features of Arduino is its built-in functions. These functions are pre- written code snippets that perform specific tasks. They are an essential aspect of programming microcontrollers and make it easier for beginners to get started.

The following are some of the most useful built-in functions in Arduino:

DigitalWrite: This function is used to control digital pins on the Arduino board. It can be used to turn a pin on or off, depending on the logic level being used.

AnalogRead: This function is used to read the value of an analog pin on the Arduino board. It converts the analog voltage into a digital value that can be used in the program.

Serial.begin: This function is used to initialize the serial communication between the Arduino board and a computer. It sets the baud rate, which is the rate at which data is transmitted between the two devices.

Delay: This function is used to pause the execution of the program for a specified amount of time. It is useful when you want to create a delay between two actions.

Random: This function is used to generate a random number between a specified range. It is useful when you want to add some random behavior to your program.

These are just a few of the many built-in functions available in Arduino. They make it easier to write codes and perform complex tasks without having to write everything from scratch.

If you are a beginner, it is important to familiarize yourself with these functions. They are the building blocks of any Arduino program and can be used to create a wide range of projects.

In addition to the built-in functions, Arduino also has a large community of developers who create libraries of code that can be used with the platform. These libraries can be used to add additional functionality to your program, such as controlling motors or sensors.

In conclusion, built-in functions are an essential aspect of programming Arduino. They make it easier for beginners to get started and provide a foundation for more complex projects. As you become more experienced with Arduino, you will likely find yourself using these functions more frequently to create innovative projects.

Creating Your Own Functions

One of the most powerful features of Arduino is the ability to create your own functions. Functions are like mini programs that can be called from within your main program.

They allow you to break up your code into smaller, more manageable pieces, making it easier to read, debug, and maintain.

To create a function, you first need to define it. This means telling Arduino what the function will be called, what parameters it will accept (if any), and what it will do. Here is an example of a simple function that adds two numbers together:

```
*********************************
int add(int a, int b) {
  return a + b;
}
*********************************
```

This function is called "add", and it takes two integer parameters, "a" and "b". It then returns the sum of the two parameters using the "+" operator.

To use this function in your main program, you would simply call it like this:

```
*********************************
int x = 5;
int y = 7;
int z = add(x, y);
*********************************
```

In this example, we define two variables, "x" and "y", and set them to the values 5 and 7, respectively. We then call the "add" function, passing in "x" and "y" as parameters. The function returns the sum of the two parameters, which we store in a third variable, "z".

You can create as many functions as you like, and they can be as complex or simple as you need them to be. Here are a few things to keep in mind when creating your own functions:

- Functions should be named descriptively, so that it is clear what they do just by looking at their name.
- Functions should have a clear purpose and should do one thing and do it well. If you find yourself creating a function that does too many things, consider breaking it up into multiple smaller functions.
- Functions should be reusable. Ideally, you should be able to call a function multiple times from various parts of your program.
- Functions can also be used to return values other than integers. For example, you could create a function that takes a string as a parameter and returns the length of that string.

By using functions, you can make your Arduino programs more modular, easier to read, and easier to maintain. Do not be afraid to experiment and create your own functions to solve the problems you encounter in your projects. With a little practice, you will soon be writing code like a pro!

Arrays

Arrays are a fundamental part of programming, and they are especially useful when working with Arduino boards. An array is a collection of data that can be accessed by an index. In simpler terms, it is like a list of variables that can be accessed with a single name.

In Arduino, arrays can be used to store data from sensors or other inputs. For example, if you have four sensors connected to your Arduino board, you can create an array to store the readings from each sensor. This will make it easier to work with the data later on.

Arrays can also be used to simplify code. Instead of creating multiple variables for similar data, you can create an array to store all the data in one place. This can make your code easier to read and maintain.

Creating an Array

To create an array in Arduino, you first need to declare the array with a name and a size. For example, to create an array that can store ten integers, you would use the following code:

int myArray[10];

This code creates an array called "myArray" that can store ten integers. The index of the first element in the array is 0, and the index of the last element is 9.

Accessing Array Elements

To access an element in an array, you need to use its index. For example, to access the third element in the "myArray" array, you would use the following code:

myArray[2];

This code returns the value stored in the third element of the array. Remember that the index of the first element is 0, so to access the third element, you need to use the index 2.

Looping Through an Array

Loops are a powerful tool in programming, and they can be used to iterate through an array. For example, if you want to print all the elements in the "myArray" array, you can use a "for" loop:

```
********************************
for (int i = 0; i < 10; i++) {
   Serial.println(myArray[i]);
}
********************************
```

This code loops through the "myArray" array and prints each element to the serial monitor. The loop starts at index 0 and continues until index 9.

Conclusion

Arrays are an essential tool in programming and can be used to store data and simplify code. In Arduino, arrays can be used to store data from sensors or other inputs, and they can be accessed with an index. By using loops, you can iterate through an array and perform operations on each element. Understanding arrays is crucial for any Arduino project, and it is a fundamental concept in programming.

Strings and "Programming with Arduino."

Strings are an essential part of programming with Arduino. They are a sequence of characters, such as letters, numbers, and symbols, which are used to represent text. Strings are commonly used to store and manipulate data in Arduino programs, such as sensor readings, user input, and output messages.

To create a string in Arduino, you must first declare it as a variable with the string data type. For example, you can declare a string variable called "message" by typing "String message;" at the beginning of your program.

You can then assign a value to the string variable by using the equal sign and enclosing the text in quotation marks, such as **"message = "Hello World!";"**

Once you have created a string variable, you can manipulate it using various string functions. For example, you can concatenate two strings together using the "+" operator, such as "message = "Hello" + "World!";" You can also find the length of a string using the "length()" function, such as "int length = message.length();"

Another useful string function is the "indexOf()" function, which allows you to find the position of a specific character or substring within a string. For example, you can find the position of the letter "o" in the string "Hello World!" by typing **"int position = message.indexOf("o");"**

Strings can also be used to receive and send data through the

Arduino's serial port. You can use the "Serial.begin()" function to start the serial communication, and the "Serial.println()" function to send a string of text to the serial port. You can also use the "Serial.available()" function to check if there is any incoming data on the serial port, and the "Serial.read()" function to read the incoming data as a string.

In conclusion, strings are a fundamental part of programming with Arduino, and are used to store and manipulate text data. Understanding how to create and manipulate strings is essential for developing Arduino programs that can communicate with users and other devices. By using various string functions, you can easily manipulate and process text data in your Arduino programs.

Working with Sensors and Actuators

Introduction to Sensors and Actuators

Sensors and actuators are essential components of any electronic system. They are used to measure and control various physical and environmental parameters, such as temperature, humidity, light, pressure, and motion. In this subchapter, we will introduce you to sensors and actuators and how they are used in Arduino projects.

Sensors

A sensor is a device that converts a physical or environmental parameter into an electrical signal that can be measured and processed by an electronic circuit. There are many types of sensors available, each with its own specific function and characteristics. Some of the most common sensors used in Arduino projects include:

1. Temperature sensor - used to measure the temperature of a specific environment.

2. Humidity sensor - used to measure the relative humidity of the

air.

3. Light sensor - used to detect the intensity of light.

4. Pressure sensor - used to measure the pressure of a fluid or gas.

5. Motion sensor - used to detect motion or movement.

Actuators

An actuator is a device that converts an electrical signal into a physical action or movement. Actuators are used to control various mechanical and electrical systems, such as motors, valves, and relays. Some of the most common actuators used in Arduino projects include:

1. Motor - used to control the movement of a mechanical system.

2. Servo - used to control the position of a mechanical system.

3. Relay - used to control the on/off state of an electrical system.

4. Solenoid - used to control the movement of a mechanical system.

Arduino and Sensors/Actuators

Arduino is an open-source platform that allows you to easily interface with sensors and actuators. The Arduino board contains analog and digital input/output pins that can be used to connect various sensors and actuators to the board. Additionally, Arduino has a vast library of code that can be used to interface with many different types of sensors and actuators.

In conclusion, sensors and actuators are critical components of any electronic system. They allow us to measure and control various physical and environmental parameters and are essential for many Arduino projects. In the next subchapter, we will introduce you to some of the most common sensors and actuators used in Arduino projects and show you how to interface them with the Arduino board.

Connecting Sensors to Arduino

Arduino boards are designed to be compatible with a wide range of sensors, making them an excellent choice for electronics enthusiasts and DIY'ers. The process of connecting sensors to Arduino is relatively straightforward and involves a few basic steps.

Step 1: Identify the Sensor

The first step is to identify the type of sensor you want to connect to your Arduino board. There are many different types of sensors available, including light sensors, temperature sensors, humidity sensors, and motion sensors, to name a few. Once you have identified the sensor, you can begin the process of connecting it to your Arduino.

Step 2: Gather the Required Components

To connect the sensor to your Arduino board, you will need several components, including the sensor itself, a breadboard, jumper wires, and a resistor if required. The resistor is typically used to limit the current flowing through the sensor and prevent damage to the Arduino board.

Step 3: Connect the Sensor to the Breadboard

The next step is to connect the sensor to the breadboard. To do this, insert the sensor's pins into the appropriate holes on the breadboard. Be sure to check the sensor's datasheet to ensure that you are connecting the pins correctly.

Step 4: Connect the Breadboard to the Arduino Board

Once you have connected the sensor to the breadboard, the next step is to connect the breadboard to the Arduino board. To do this, use jumper wires to connect the sensor's pins to the appropriate pins on the Arduino board. Again, be sure to check the sensor's datasheet to ensure that you are connecting the pins correctly.

Step 5: Write the Code

The last step is to write the code that will allow your Arduino board to communicate with the sensor. This involves using the Arduino Integrated Development Environment (IDE) to write a few lines of code that will read the sensor's output and display it on your computer screen. There are many tutorials available online that can guide you through the process of writing code for different types of sensors.

In conclusion, connecting sensors to Arduino is a straightforward process that requires a few basic components and some coding skills. By following the steps outlined above, you can quickly and easily connect diverse types of sensors to your Arduino board and begin experimenting with different projects.

Reading Sensor Data

One of the most exciting and useful features of Arduino is its ability to read sensor data. Sensors are devices that can detect changes in the environment and convert them into electrical signals that can be read by the microcontroller on the Arduino board. There are many types of sensors available, including temperature sensors, light sensors, motion sensors, and more.

To read sensor data with Arduino, you will need to connect the sensor to one of the input pins on the board. The exact pin you use will depend on the type of sensor you are using and how it is wired. Once the sensor is connected, you can use Arduino's built-in functions to read the data and perform actions based on the results.

For example, let us say you want to use a temperature sensor to control a fan. You could connect the sensor to the analog input pin A0 on the Arduino board and then use the following code to read the temperature data:

```
*********************************
int sensorValue = analogRead(A0);
float voltage = sensorValue * (5.0 / 1023.0);
float temperature = (voltage - 0.5) * 100;
*********************************
```

In this code, we first read the analog input value from pin A0 using the `analogRead()` function. We then convert the value to a voltage using a simple formula, and finally, we calculate the temperature based on the voltage using another formula. This code assumes that the temperature sensor is wired to provide a voltage that varies linearly with temperature, which is the case for many types of temperature sensors.

Once you have the temperature data, you can use it to control the fan by turning it on or off based on a threshold temperature. You could use a simple `if` statement like this:

```
********************************
if (temperature > 25) {
  digitalWrite(9, HIGH);
} else {
  digitalWrite(9, LOW);
}
********************************
```

In this code, we check if the temperature is greater than 25 degrees Celsius. If it is, we turn on the fan by setting pin 9 to a high voltage. If it is not, we turn off the fan by setting pin 9 to a low voltage.

This is just one example of how you can use Arduino to read sensor data and perform actions based on the results. With a little creativity and experimentation, you can use sensors to create all sorts of interesting and useful projects.

Using Actuators

Actuators are devices that can control physical movement or action. These devices can be used in a wide range of applications, from robotics to home automation. In Arduino projects, actuators are often used to create motion or change the state of a physical object.

In this section, we will discuss the different types of actuators that can be used with Arduino and how to control them.

Types of Actuators

There are several types of actuators that can be used with Arduino, including:

1. **Servo Motors** – These are small motors that can rotate to a specific angle. They are commonly used in robotics and can be controlled using PWM signals.

2. **Stepper Motors** – These are motors that can move in precise steps, making them ideal for positioning applications. They can be controlled using a variety of methods, including using a stepper motor driver board.

3. **DC Motors** – These are motors that can rotate in either

direction and can be controlled using PWM signals.

4. **Solenoids** – These are devices that can create linear motion and are often used in locking mechanisms or valves.

Controlling Actuators with Arduino

To control actuators with Arduino, you will need to connect them to the appropriate pins on the board. For example, servo motors can be connected to the PWM pins, while DC motors can be connected to the digital pins using a motor controller.

Once the actuators are connected to the board, you can use code to control their movement. For example, to control a servo motor, you can use the Servo library in Arduino to set the angle of rotation. To control a DC motor, you can use PWM signals to adjust the speed and direction of rotation.

Conclusion

Actuators are important components of many Arduino projects and can be used to create a wide range of motion and action. By understanding the diverse types of actuators and how to control them with Arduino, you can take your projects to the next level and create dynamic and interactive devices.

LEDs

LEDs (Light Emitting Diodes) are an essential component in electronics and have become increasingly popular in recent years. They are used in a wide range of applications, from lighting to electronic displays. In this subchapter, we will discuss the basics of LEDs and how to use them with an Arduino.

What are LEDs?

LEDs are semiconductor diodes that emit light when a current passes through them. They are made of semiconductor materials that emit photons when an electrical current passes through them. Unlike incandescent bulbs, LEDs do not have a filament that can burn out, making them more durable and long-lasting. LEDs are available in different colors, including red, green, blue, yellow, and white.

How do LEDs work?

LEDs have two terminals, an anode (+) and a cathode (-). When a voltage is applied across the terminals, electrons flow from the anode to the cathode, causing the LED to emit light. The color of the light emitted depends on the type of semiconductor material used in the LED.

Using LEDs with an Arduino

To use LEDs with an Arduino, you need to connect them to one of the digital pins on the board. You can use either a resistor or a transistor to control the current flowing through the LED. The resistor limits the current and prevents the LED from burning out, while the transistor acts as a switch that can turn the LED on and off.

To turn an LED on and off using an Arduino, you need to write a simple code that sends a signal to the digital pin. Here is an example code that turns an LED on and off:

```
********************************
void setup() {
  pinMode(13, OUTPUT);
}

void loop() {
  digitalWrite(13, HIGH);
  delay(1000);
  digitalWrite(13, LOW);
  delay(1000);
}
********************************
```

This code sets pin 13 as an output and then turns the LED on and off with a delay of 1 second between each state change.

Conclusion

LEDs are a versatile and cost-effective component that can be used in a wide range of electronic projects. They are easy to use with an Arduino and can be controlled with simple code. Whether you are a beginner in electronics or an experienced DIY'er, LEDs are a 'must- have' component in your toolkit.

Motors

Motors are a crucial element of many electronic projects and are essential for controlling movement. Whether you are building a robot, a remote-controlled vehicle, or a simple motorized toy, understanding how to control motors with an Arduino is a foundational skill for any electronics enthusiast or DIY'er.

Arduino microprocessors provide an ideal platform for controlling motors due to their versatility and ease of use. With a few lines of code, you can control different types of motors, including DC motors, stepper motors, and servo motors, to perform a wide range of tasks.

DC motors are the most common type of motor used in electronic projects. They are relatively simple to control and can be used for a variety of applications. To control a DC motor with an Arduino, you will need a motor driver, which is a circuit that allows the microprocessor to control the motor's speed and direction. There are many types of motor drivers available, ranging from basic H-bridge drivers to more advanced integrated circuits.

Stepper motors are also widely used in electronics projects and are ideal for precise movement control. Stepper motors move in small, precise steps rather than continuously rotating. To control a stepper motor with an Arduino, you will need a stepper motor driver, which converts the signals from the microprocessor into the correct sequence of signals for the motor.

Servo motors are used in robotics and other applications where precise control of movement is required. Unlike DC or stepper motors, servo motors have a built-in feedback mechanism that allows them to maintain a specific position. To control a servo motor with an Arduino, you simply need to send a signal indicating the desired position, and the motor will move to that position and hold it.

In conclusion, motors are an essential component for many electronic projects, and Arduino microprocessors provide an ideal platform for controlling them. Whether you are working with DC, stepper, or servo motors, understanding how to control them with an Arduino will give you the skills you need to create a wide range of exciting projects.

Servos

Servos are one of the most commonly used devices in the field of robotics and automation. They are also an integral part of the Arduino platform and understanding how they work is essential for any electronics enthusiast or DIY'er looking to create their own projects.

A servo is essentially a small motor that is capable of rotating to a specific angle. They are controlled by a series of pulses sent from an Arduino or other microcontroller, which tells the servo how far to rotate. These pulses are typically sent at a frequency of around 50 Hz, with the duration of each pulse controlling the position of the servo.

There are two main types of servos: continuous rotation and standard servos. Continuous rotation servos are capable of rotating continuously in either direction, while standard servos are limited to a specific range of motion, typically between 0 and 180 degrees.

To use a servo with an Arduino, you will need to connect it to one of the digital pins on the board. The wiring is simple, with the servo typically requiring power, ground, and a signal wire. The signal wire is connected to the digital pin on the Arduino, while the power and ground wires are connected to the appropriate pins on the board.

Once your servo is connected, you can begin controlling it with your Arduino code. The Servo library in Arduino makes it easy to control your servo, with simple commands like servo.write(angle) allowing you to set the position of the servo.

Overall, servos are an essential component of any Arduino project that involves robotics or automation. With a basic understanding of how they work and how to control them with Arduino, you can begin creating your own projects that incorporate these powerful devices.

Controlling Multiple Actuators

Actuators are devices that convert electrical signals to physical movements. Examples of actuators include motors, solenoids, and relays. In most Arduino projects, multiple actuators are required to perform a specific task. However, controlling multiple actuators simultaneously can be challenging, especially for beginners.

The good news is that the Arduino board can control

multiple actuators by using simple programming techniques. The key is to use a technique called multiplexing. Multiplexing is a way of controlling multiple devices using a single pin or a set of pins. It involves switching between the devices to activate them one at a time.

There are different types of multiplexing techniques, including time-division multiplexing (TDM), frequency-division multiplexing (FDM), and code-division multiplexing (CDM). However, the most used technique for controlling multiple actuators with Arduino is called the multiplexed display.

The multiplexed display technique involves connecting multiple LEDs to a single pin or a set of pins on the Arduino board. The LEDs are then turned on and off one at a time in a rapid sequence to create the illusion of a continuous display. This technique can be extended to control other types of actuators, such as motors and relays.

To control multiple actuators using the multiplexed display technique, you will need to use a shift register. A shift register is a device that can store and shift data serially. It allows you to control multiple outputs using only a few pins on the Arduino board.

To use a shift register, you will need to connect it to the Arduino board and the actuators. You will also need to write a program that sends data to the shift register and controls the actuators based on the data.

In conclusion, controlling multiple actuators with Arduino is possible using the multiplexed display technique and a shift register. This technique allows you to control multiple devices using only a few pins on the Arduino board. With some practice, you can use this technique to create complex projects that involve multiple actuators and sensors.

Building Interactive Projects

Introduction to Interactive Projects

Interactive projects are an exciting way to explore the world of electronics and programming. With the help of Arduino, you can create projects that respond to user input, interact with the environment, and even communicate with other devices.

In this chapter, we will introduce you to the concept of interactive projects and show you some examples of what you can do with Arduino. We will also cover the basic components that you will need to get started.

Interactive projects are those that respond to user input or the environment in some way. For example, you could create a project that lights up when someone enters a room, or a project that plays a sound when a button is pressed. The possibilities are endless.

The key to creating interactive projects is programming. With Arduino, you can write code that controls the behavior of your project. You can use sensors to detect changes in the environment, and actuator devices to respond to those changes.

One of the remarkable things about Arduino is that it is easy to learn and use. Even if you have no programming experience, you can quickly get up to speed with the basics. There are plenty of resources available online, including tutorials, videos, and forums, where you can get help and advice from other Arduino enthusiasts.

To get started with interactive projects, you will need a few basic components. These include an Arduino board, sensors (such as light sensors or temperature sensors), actuators (such as LEDs or motors), and some basic electronic components such as resistors and capacitors.

In the following chapters, we will show you how to use these components to create some simple interactive projects, such as a light sensor that turns on an LED when it gets dark, or a temperature sensor that controls a fan. With practice, you can move on to more complex projects, such as robots or home automation systems.

In summary, interactive projects are a fun and engaging way to explore the world of electronics and programming. With Arduino, you can create projects that respond to user input and the environment, and the possibilities are endless. In the next chapters, we will show you how to get started with some basic projects, and help you develop the skills and knowledge to tackle more complex projects in the future.

Building a Simple Game

Arduino is not just a tool for controlling electronic devices or monitoring sensors. With a little bit of programming and creativity, you can also use Arduino to create fun and interactive games. In this subchapter, we will show you how to build a simple game using Arduino.

The game we will create is called the "Reaction Time Game." The objective of the game is to press a button as soon as an LED turns on. The faster you press the button, the higher your score. Here are the materials you will need to build the game:

- Arduino Uno board
- Breadboard
- LED
- Push button
- Resistor (220 ohms)
- Jumper wires

Step 1: Connect the LED and the resistor to the Arduino board. Connect the anode (positive) pin of the LED to pin 13 of the Arduino board. Connect the cathode (negative) pin of the LED to one end of the resistor. Connect the other end of the resistor to the ground (GND) pin of the Arduino board.

Step 2: Connect the push button to the Arduino board. Connect one of the legs of the push button to pin 2 of the Arduino board. Connect the other leg of the push button to the ground (GND) pin of the Arduino board.

Step 3: Upload the following code to the Arduino board:

```
********************************
int ledPin = 13;
int buttonPin = 2;
int score = 0;
boolean isPressed = false;
long startTime = 0;
long reactionTime = 0;

void setup() {
  pinMode(ledPin, OUTPUT);
  pinMode(buttonPin, INPUT_PULLUP);
  randomSeed(analogRead(0));
  Serial.begin(9600);
}

void loop() {
  digitalWrite(ledPin, HIGH);
  delay(random(1000, 5000));
  digitalWrite(ledPin, LOW);
```

```
while (digitalRead(buttonPin) == HIGH) {
  isPressed = true;
  startTime = millis();
}

while (digitalRead(buttonPin) == LOW) {
  reactionTime = millis() - startTime;
  score = 10000 / reactionTime;
  Serial.print("Your score: ");
  Serial.println(score);
  delay(1000);
}
}
}
```
****

Step 4: Open the Serial Monitor in the Arduino IDE to see your score. Press the reset button on the Arduino board to restart the game.

Congratulations! You have just built a simple game using Arduino. Feel free to modify the game by changing the LED blink time or adding more buttons. Have fun!

Creating a Weather Station

One of the most exciting projects you can undertake as an electronics enthusiast is building your own weather station. With an Arduino board and a few sensors, you can create a device that measures temperature, humidity, and atmospheric pressure. The data collected can be displayed on an LCD screen or transmitted wirelessly to a computer or smartphone.

To begin, you will need an Arduino board and a few sensors. The three sensors you will need are a temperature sensor, a humidity sensor, and a barometric pressure sensor. There are many different types of sensors available, but the DHT11 and DHT22 are popular choices for temperature and humidity, while the BMP180 is a reliable barometric pressure sensor.

Once you have your sensors, you will need to connect them to your Arduino board. Each sensor will have its own set of pins that need to be connected to the appropriate pins on the board. The temperature and humidity sensors will typically have three pins: power, ground, and data. The barometric pressure sensor will have four pins: power, ground, data, and clock.

Once your sensors are connected, you will need to write the

code to read the data from each sensor and display it on the LCD screen or transmit it wirelessly. You can use the Arduino IDE to write the code, which is a simple programming language that is easy to learn.

To display the data on an LCD screen, you will need to connect the screen to the Arduino board and write code to display the data. Alternatively, you can use a wireless module like the ESP8266 to transmit the data to a computer or smartphone.

When building a weather station, it is important to consider the placement of the sensors. The temperature and humidity sensors should be placed in a shaded area away from direct sunlight and sources of heat. The barometric pressure sensor should be placed in an area with good airflow and away from sources of heat or cold.

In conclusion, building a weather station with an Arduino board is a fun and educational project for electronics enthusiasts. With a few sensors and some basic programming skills, you can create a device that measures temperature, humidity, and atmospheric pressure. The data collected can be displayed on an LCD screen or transmitted wirelessly, making it a great tool for monitoring weather conditions.

Building a Security System

As an electronics enthusiast and a do-it-yourselfer, building a security system using Arduino can be a fun and rewarding project. With the help of Arduino, you can create a custom security system that suits your needs and preferences. In this chapter, we will guide you through the steps to build a simple and effective security system using Arduino.

The security system we will be building will consist of three main components: a motion sensor, a buzzer, and an LED. The motion sensor will detect any movement in its vicinity and send a signal to the Arduino board. The Arduino board will then activate the buzzer and the LED to alert you of the potential threat.

To begin building the security system, you will need the following components:

- Arduino Uno board
- Breadboard
- Motion sensor
- Buzzer
- LED
- Jumper wires

Firstly, connect the motion sensor to the breadboard using the jumper wires. Connect the power supply and the ground of the motion sensor to the power and ground rails on the breadboard, respectively. Connect the signal pin of the motion sensor to digital pin 2 on the Arduino board.

Next, connect the buzzer to the breadboard and connect one of its pins to digital pin 3 on the Arduino board. Connect the other pin of the buzzer to the ground rail on the breadboard.

Finally, connect the LED to the breadboard and connect its positive pin to digital pin 4 on the Arduino board. Connect the negative pin of the LED to the ground rail on the breadboard.

Now that all the components are connected, you can upload the code to the Arduino board. The code will read the signal from the motion sensor and activate the buzzer and the LED when motion is detected. You can customize the code to suit your preferences, such as changing the duration of the buzzer or the brightness of the LED.

In conclusion, building a security system using Arduino is a fantastic way to explore the possibilities of electronics and programming. With a few simple components and some basic coding, you can create a custom security system that meets your needs and preferences. We hope this chapter has inspired you to start your own security system project using Arduino.

Designing a Smart Home System

Smart homes are becoming increasingly popular and are transforming the way we live. With the help of technology, we can control and automate various aspects of our homes, such as lighting, temperature, security, and entertainment. In this subchapter, we will discuss how to design a smart home system using Arduino.

Before getting started, it is essential to understand the components required for building a smart home system. The following are the primary components:

```
*********************************
void loop() {
  digitalWrite(ledPin, HIGH);
  delay(random(1000, 5000));
  digitalWrite(ledPin, LOW);

  while (digitalRead(buttonPin) == HIGH) {
    isPressed = true;
    startTime = millis();
  }

  while (digitalRead(buttonPin) == LOW) {
    reactionTime = millis() - startTime;
```

```
    score = 10000 / reactionTime;
    Serial.print("Your score: ");
    Serial.println(score);
    delay(1000);
  }
}
```
****

Arduino board: An Arduino board is a microcontroller that acts as the brain of the system. It is responsible for controlling and communicating with other components of the system.

1. **Sensors:** Sensors are used to detect changes in the environment. For example, temperature sensors can detect the temperature of a room, and motion sensors can detect movement.

2. **Actuators:** Actuators are used to control devices. For example, a relay can be used to control the lights in a room, and a motor can be used to open and close a door.

3. **Communication modules:** Communication modules are used to establish communication between the Arduino board and other devices. For example, a Wi-Fi module can be used to connect the system to the internet.

Once you have the components, you can start designing the system. The first step is to identify the devices you want to control. For example, you may want to control the lights, fans, and air conditioning in your home.

Next, you need to identify the sensors required to automate the system. For example, you may want to use a temperature sensor to control the air conditioning.

After that, you need to identify the actuators required to control the devices. For example, you may want to use a relay to control the lights.

Once you have identified the components, you can start programming the Arduino board. The programming involves writing code to control the sensors and actuators and establish communication between the devices.

In conclusion, designing a smart home system using Arduino requires careful planning and programming. By following the steps outlined in this subchapter, you can design a system that meets your specific needs and transforms your home into a smart home.

Advanced Arduino Topics

Interfacing with Other Devices

In today's world, electronic devices have become the backbone of our lives. From smartphones to smart homes, everything we use is connected to each other. This concept of connectivity is not only limited to devices, but it also extends to microcontrollers like Arduino. With Arduino, you can connect and interface with other devices to create a more complex and interactive system.

Interfacing with other devices is a crucial aspect of the Arduino ecosystem. It allows you to expand the capabilities of the Arduino board and create more diverse projects. Some of the devices that you can interface with Arduino include sensors, actuators, displays, and communication modules.

One of the most common devices that you can interface with Arduino is a sensor. Sensors are used to detect and measure various environmental conditions such as light, temperature, humidity, and motion. Arduino boards have analog and digital pins that can be used to read sensor values. You can use libraries and code examples available online to connect and read data from the sensor.

Another device that you can interface with Arduino is an actuator. Actuators are devices that perform a physical action based on the input received. Examples of actuators include motors, servos, and relays. You can use Arduino to control the movement of these devices by sending signals to them through the digital pins.

Displays are another type of device that you can interface with Arduino. Displays are used to visualize data and information. Common types of displays that you can use with Arduino include LCD and OLED displays. You can use libraries and code examples available online to display text, images, and other types of data on these displays.

Finally, communication modules are devices that allow Arduino to communicate with other devices and systems. Examples of communication modules include Bluetooth and Wi-Fi modules. These modules allow you to connect your Arduino board to the internet or other devices wirelessly.

In conclusion, interfacing with other devices is an essential aspect of the Arduino ecosystem. It allows you to create more diverse and interactive projects. By connecting sensors, actuators, displays, and communication modules, you can expand the capabilities of your Arduino board and create more complex systems.

Bluetooth

Bluetooth technology has revolutionized the way we connect and communicate with our devices. It is a wireless technology that allows devices to communicate with one another over short distances. The technology uses radio waves to transmit data between devices, making it an ideal technology for IoT (Internet of Things) devices.

Arduino boards are equipped with Bluetooth modules, which make it easy to connect your Arduino board to other devices using Bluetooth. The Bluetooth module allows you to send and receive data wirelessly between your Arduino board and other devices such as smartphones, laptops, and tablets.

To use Bluetooth with your Arduino board, you will need to have a Bluetooth module. There are several types of Bluetooth modules available, but the most commonly used one is the HC-05 module. This module is easy to use and is compatible with most Arduino boards.

To use the HC-05 Bluetooth module, you will need to connect it to your Arduino board. The module has four pins that need to be connected to the Arduino board. The pins are VCC, GND, TX, and RX. The module is powered by the Arduino board's 5V pin, and the GND pin is connected to the ground pin on the

Arduino board.

Once the module is connected to the Arduino board, you can start using it to communicate with other devices using Bluetooth. You can use the Bluetooth module to control your Arduino board remotely using a smartphone or tablet. You can also use it to send data from your Arduino board to other devices, such as temperature readings or sensor data.

In conclusion, Bluetooth technology is a terrific way to connect your Arduino board to other devices wirelessly. With the HC-05 Bluetooth module, you can easily connect your Arduino board to other devices and start communicating wirelessly. Bluetooth technology is an important part of IoT and is a wonderful way to take your electronics projects to the next level.

Wi-Fi

In today's world, Wi-Fi is an important part of our daily lives. From streaming movies to browsing the internet, we rely on Wi-Fi for almost everything. As an electronics enthusiast or a DIY'er, it is essential to understand how Wi-Fi works and how it can be integrated with Arduino.

Wi-Fi stands for Wireless Fidelity and refers to a wireless networking technology that uses radio waves to provide wireless high-speed internet and network connections. Wi-Fi operates on a frequency of 2.4GHz or 5GHz and has a range of up to 300 feet, depending on the environment.

To use Wi-Fi with Arduino, you need a Wi-Fi shield or a Wi-Fi module. Shields are add-on boards that sit on top of the Arduino board and provide additional functionality. Wi-Fi shields are designed to provide wireless internet connectivity to your Arduino projects. They have an onboard Wi-Fi module that connects to your local Wi-Fi network and allows your Arduino to communicate with other devices connected to the same network.

A popular Wi-Fi shield for Arduino is the ESP8266, which is a low-cost Wi-Fi module that can be easily integrated with Arduino. The ESP8266 can be programmed using the Arduino IDE and can be used to create a wide range of Wi-Fi-enabled projects. Some of the popular applications of ESP8266 include home automation, IoT projects, and smart devices.

To use the ESP8266 with Arduino, you need to install the ESP8266 board package in the Arduino IDE. Once installed, you can select the ESP8266 board from the board menu and program it just like any other Arduino board.

In conclusion, Wi-Fi is an essential technology that can be easily integrated with Arduino to create a wide range of projects. With the help of Wi-Fi shields and modules, you can connect your Arduino to the internet and communicate with other devices on the same network. The ESP8266 is a popular Wi-Fi module that can be easily integrated with Arduino and offers a wide range of applications. As an electronics enthusiast or a DIY'er, understanding the basics of Wi-Fi and its integration with Arduino can open up a whole new world of possibilities.

Ethernet

Ethernet is a type of networking protocol that is used to connect devices to a network. It is widely used in homes, offices, and industries to connect devices like computers, printers, and servers to a network. The protocol is based on the Ethernet standard, which was first introduced by Xerox in the 1970s. Ethernet is a wired networking technology, which means that it requires a physical connection between devices.

Ethernet is a powerful tool for electronics enthusiasts and do-it-yourselfers who are looking to create and connect their own devices to a network. With Ethernet, you can easily connect your Arduino board to the internet and control it remotely from any location.

To connect your Arduino board to Ethernet, you will need an Ethernet shield, which is a small circuit board that fits over your Arduino board and provides Ethernet connectivity. The shield includes an Ethernet controller chip, which handles the communication between your Arduino board and the network.

Once you have your Ethernet shield installed, you can begin programming your Arduino board to communicate with the network. One of the most common applications of Ethernet with Arduino is to create an Internet of Things (IoT) device. An IoT device is a device that can be controlled or monitored remotely over the internet.

For example, you could create an IoT temperature sensor using an Arduino board and an Ethernet shield. The temperature sensor could be placed in a remote location, such as a greenhouse or a server room, and the data could be transmitted over the internet to a central control system.

Overall, Ethernet is a powerful tool for electronics enthusiasts and do-it-yourselfers who are looking to create and connect their own devices to a network. With Ethernet, you can easily connect your Arduino board to the internet and control it remotely from any location.

Memory Management

In the world of electronics, memory management is an important concept to understand. This is especially true when it comes to programming microcontrollers like the Arduino. In this subchapter, we will take a closer look at memory management and how it applies to the Arduino platform.

At its core, memory management is all about allocating and deallocating memory resources. In the context of the Arduino, this means making sure that the microcontroller has enough memory to run your program. The Arduino has two types of memory: Flash memory and SRAM.

Flash memory is where your program code is stored. This is a non-volatile memory, meaning that it retains its contents even when the power is turned off. This is important because it allows your program to continue running even after the Arduino is turned off and then back on again.

SRAM, on the other hand, is where your program variables are stored. This is a volatile memory, meaning that its contents are lost when the power is turned off. It is important to keep track of the amount of SRAM being used by your program because if you use too much, your program may crash or behave unpredictably.

To manage memory on the Arduino, you need to be aware of a few key concepts. First, you need to make sure that your program is not using more memory than the Arduino has available. This means carefully managing your program variables and making sure that you are not allocating more memory than you need.

Second, you need to be aware of how your program is using memory over time. For example, if your program has a loop that runs repeatedly, you need to make sure that it is not allocating and deallocating memory every time it runs. This can lead to memory fragmentation, which can cause your program to crash or behave unpredictably.

Finally, you need to be aware of any libraries or external code that your program is using. These libraries may allocate memory on their own, and you need to make sure that they are not using more memory than you have available.

In conclusion, memory management is a critical concept to understand when programming the Arduino. By carefully managing your program variables and being aware of how your program uses memory over time, you can ensure that your program runs smoothly and reliably.

Interrupts

Interrupts are a crucial aspect of Arduino programming that every beginner must understand. An interrupt is a signal that notifies the microcontroller to stop its current task and attend to a higher priority task. Interrupts allow the Arduino to respond to external events, such as button presses, sensor readings, or communication requests, without having to wait for the current task to finish.

There are two types of interrupts in Arduino: external interrupts and timer interrupts. External interrupts are triggered by external events, such as a button press or a sensor reading. When an external interrupt occurs, the microcontroller stops its current task and jumps to the interrupt service routine (ISR) to execute the code associated with the interrupt. External interrupts can be enabled on any of the Arduino's digital pins and can be configured to trigger on a rising edge, falling edge, or both.

Timer interrupts, on the other hand, are triggered by a timer that runs independently of the main program. Timer interrupts are useful for timing events, such as controlling the speed of a motor or generating a pulse train. When a timer interrupt occurs, the microcontroller jumps to the ISR to execute the code associated with the interrupt. Timer interrupts can be configured to occur at regular intervals or set to trigger at a specific time.

Interrupts are essential for real-time applications, where timing and responsiveness are critical. By using interrupts, the Arduino can respond to external events with minimal delay, ensuring that the system operates smoothly and efficiently. Interrupts also allow the Arduino to perform multiple tasks simultaneously, making it possible to control several devices or sensors at once.

To use interrupts in your Arduino projects, you need to understand how to write interrupt service routines and how to configure the interrupt settings. You also need to be aware of the potential pitfalls of using interrupts, such as interrupt conflicts and race conditions. However, with a little practice and patience, you can become proficient in using interrupts and take your Arduino projects to the next level.

In conclusion, interrupts are an essential aspect of Arduino programming that every beginner must understand. They allow the Arduino to respond to external events, perform multiple tasks simultaneously and ensure that the system operates smoothly and efficiently. By learning how to use interrupts, you can take your Arduino projects to the next level and create more complex and sophisticated applications.

Debugging and Troubleshooting

As with any electronic project, debugging and troubleshooting are essential skills for any Arduino enthusiast. Debugging is the process of identifying and fixing errors or bugs in your code, while troubleshooting involves identifying and fixing hardware issues in your Arduino project.

Debugging

When debugging your Arduino project, start by checking your code for syntax errors. Syntax errors are the most common cause of bugs in Arduino projects. Make sure that your code is properly formatted, and that you have closed all your parentheses, brackets, and quotes.

Next, use the Serial Monitor to print out debug messages that will help you identify where your code is failing. The Serial Monitor is a powerful tool that allows you to send and receive data between your Arduino and your computer. By adding print statements in your code, you can output data to the Serial Monitor and see what is happening in your code in real-time.

Another useful debugging tool is the LED. You can use an LED to indicate when a particular section of your code is being executed. By placing an LED in the circuit and turning it on when a particular line of code is executed, you can visually see where your code is failing.

Troubleshooting

When troubleshooting your Arduino project, start by checking your wiring and connections. Make sure that all your wires are properly connected, and that your components are correctly placed on the breadboard.

If you are having trouble with a particular component, try replacing it with a known-good component. This will help you identify if the problem is with the component or with your circuit.

If you are still having trouble, use a multimeter to check for continuity and voltage. A multimeter is an essential tool for any electronics enthusiast, and it can help you identify where the problem is in your circuit.

Conclusion

Debugging and troubleshooting are essential skills for any Arduino enthusiast. By following these tips and using the right tools, you can quickly identify and fix any issues in your Arduino project. Remember to always double-check your code and wiring, and do not be afraid to ask for help if you need it. With practice, you will become an expert at debugging and troubleshooting, and you will be able to tackle even the most complex Arduino projects with ease.

Power Management

Power management is an important aspect of any electronic project, and it is no exception when it comes to working with Arduino boards. As Arduino boards are designed to be used in a wide range of projects, from simple LED blinking to complex robotics, it is important to have a good understanding of power management techniques to ensure that your project runs efficiently and reliably.

One of the first things to consider when working with Arduino is the power source. Arduino boards can be powered in a variety of ways, including through USB, batteries, or a power supply. The type of power source you choose will depend on the specific requirements of your project and the components you are using.

When it comes to power consumption, Arduino boards are relatively low-power devices. However, the amount of power they consume can still be a concern, particularly if you are using a battery-powered project. To reduce power consumption, there are a few key things you can do:

- Use sleep modes: Arduino boards have built-in sleep modes that allow them to conserve power when they are not actively doing anything. By using sleep modes, you can significantly reduce power consumption.
- Use efficient components: When choosing components for your project, look for ones that are designed to be energy efficient. For example, LED lights that are designed to be low-power will consume less energy than standard LED lights.
- Use power regulators: If you are using a battery as your power source, it is important to use a power regulator to ensure that the voltage remains stable. This will prevent your components from drawing too much power and potentially damaging your

battery.

Another important aspect of power management is understanding how to measure and monitor power consumption. Arduino boards have built-in functions that allow you to measure the voltage and current that are being used by your project. By monitoring these measurements, you can identify areas where you may be using too much power and make necessary adjustments to reduce consumption.

In conclusion, power management is an essential aspect of any electronic project, and Arduino is no exception. By understanding the different power sources available, using efficient components, and monitoring power consumption, you can ensure that your project runs smoothly and efficiently.

Conclusion

Recap of What You Have Learned

Congratulations on making it this far! You have learned a lot about Arduino and electronics, and you should be proud of yourself. In this recap, we will briefly go over some of the main points you have learned throughout this book.

Firstly, you learned about the basics of electronics, including voltage, current, and resistance. You also learned about Ohm's Law, which is a fundamental principle of electronics that helps you calculate the relationship between these variables.

Next, you learned about the Arduino board, including its various components, such as the microcontroller, USB port, and power supply. You also learned how to install the Arduino IDE (Integrated Development Environment) on your computer, which is the software you use to write and upload code to the Arduino board.

You then learned how to write your first program, or "sketch," in the Arduino IDE. This included using basic programming concepts such as variables, functions, and loops. You also learned how to use digital and analog input and output pins on the Arduino board to control LEDs, motors, and other electronic components.

You also learned about more advanced topics, such as serial communication, which allows you to send and receive data between the Arduino board and other devices, such as sensors and displays. You also learned about using libraries, which are pre-written sets of code that make it easier to use complex components and functions in your projects.

Finally, you learned about some of the many projects you can create with Arduino, from simple LED blinkers to more complex robots and home automation systems. You also learned about some of the resources available to help you continue learning and building with Arduino, including online forums and communities, books, and courses.

Overall, you have learned a lot about electronics and Arduino, and you should be proud of your progress. Keep practicing and experimenting, and you will be well on your way to becoming an Arduino expert!

Tips for Further Learning

Congratulations! You have made it through the basic concepts of Arduino and have successfully completed your first project(s). But do not stop here! There are still many more things to learn about Arduino and electronics in general. Here are some tips for further learning that you may find helpful.

1. Join online communities: The internet is a great resource for learning about Arduino and electronics. Joining online communities such as forums or social media groups can help you connect with other enthusiasts, share ideas, and get answers to your questions.

2. Read books and tutorials: While hands-on experience is important, reading books and tutorials can provide you with a deeper understanding of electronics and Arduino. There are plenty of free resources available online, and books can be purchased at your local library or bookstore.

3. Attend workshops and events: Attending workshops and events can be a wonderful way to learn about recent technologies, meet other enthusiasts, and get hands-on experience with new tools and equipment. Look for events in your area or online.

4. Experiment with different sensors and components: Once you have become comfortable with basic Arduino projects, start experimenting with different sensors and components to expand your knowledge. There are many sensors available that

can be used for a variety of projects, such as temperature sensors, light sensors, and motion sensors.

5. Build your own projects: The best way to learn is by doing, so start building your own projects. Start with small projects and work your way up to more complex ones. Do not be afraid to try new things and make mistakes – that is how you learn!

6. Collaborate with others: Collaborating with others can help you learn new skills and get feedback on your projects. Join a local makerspace or create your own group to share ideas and work on projects together.

Remember, learning about electronics and Arduino is a never-ending process. Keep exploring, experimenting, and building to expand your knowledge and skills. Happy tinkering!

Final Thoughts

Congratulations! You have made it to the end of Arduino 101: A Beginner's Guide to Arduino Design and Programming. We hope that this book has been helpful in providing you with a solid foundation for understanding the basics of electronics and the Arduino platform.

As you have learned, Arduino is a powerful tool that can be used to build a wide range of electronic projects. It is a fantastic platform for beginners who want to learn about electronics and programming, but it is also a favorite among experienced makers who want to build complex projects quickly and easily.

We have covered a lot of ground in this book, from the basics of electronics, through the programming concepts you need to master in order to work with Arduino, and finally to some of the more advanced projects you can build with this platform.

But this is just the beginning. There is so much more to learn about electronics and Arduino. We encourage you to keep learning and experimenting. Do not be afraid to try new things and make mistakes – that is how you learn!

Some final tips for electronics enthusiasts and do-it-yourselfers who are just starting out with Arduino:

1. **Join a community:** There is a vibrant community of Arduino users out there, and they are always willing to help. Join a forum or a local makerspace to connect with other enthusiasts, share your projects, and get help when you need it.

2. **Keep it simple:** When you are just starting out, it is easy to get overwhelmed by the possibilities of Arduino. But remember, you do not need to build a robot or a smart home system right away. Start with simple projects and work your way up.

3. **Have fun:** Arduino is a great platform for building things that you are passionate about. Whether it is a game console, a musical instrument, or a home automation system, make sure you are having fun while you are doing it.

We hope that you have enjoyed learning about Arduino and electronics with us. Good luck with your future projects, and happy making!

Appendices

Glossary of Arduino Terms

The Glossary of Arduino Terms is an essential reference for any electronics enthusiast or DIY'er looking to delve into the world of Arduino. This section is designed to provide a comprehensive list of commonly used terms and definitions, so that beginners can become familiar with the language of Arduino.

Arduino: An open-source hardware and software platform that can be used to create interactive electronic projects.

Board: The physical circuit board that houses the microcontroller, components, and connectors needed to run an Arduino project.

Microcontroller: A small computer on a single integrated circuit that is used to control the behavior of an electronic device.

Programming Language: The language used to write code for Arduino projects. Arduino uses a simplified version of C++.

Shield: A board that can be plugged into an Arduino board to provide additional functionality and features.

Serial Communication: The process of sending and receiving data between a computer and an Arduino board.

Input: Signals or data received by an Arduino board from sensors, switches, or other electronic devices.

Output: Signals or data sent by an Arduino board to control external devices such as LEDs, motors, and displays.

Digital Pin: A pin on an Arduino board that can be used to read or write digital signals (either on or off).

Analog Pin: A pin on an Arduino board that can be used to read analog signals (varying voltage levels).

PWM (Pulse Width Modulation): A technique used to control the intensity of a digital signal by varying the duty cycle of the signal.

Library: A collection of pre-written code that can be used to simplify the programming of an Arduino project.

Sketch: The term used to describe the code written in the Arduino programming language.

These are just a few of the many terms that you will encounter when working with Arduino. By becoming familiar with these terms and their definitions, you will be better equipped to understand the language of Arduino and start building your own projects.

Recommended Resources

As you start your journey with Arduino, it is essential to have the right resources to help you learn and make the most of the platform. In this subchapter, we will introduce you to some of the recommended resources that can help you get started with Arduino.

1. Arduino Starter Kit

If you are new to Arduino, we recommend you start with the Arduino Starter Kit. It is a comprehensive kit that includes all the necessary components, such as a board, sensors, and actuators. The kit comes with a detailed guidebook that will help you build 15 projects from scratch.

2. Arduino Forum

Arduino Forum is a great place to connect with other Arduino enthusiasts and ask for help. You can post your questions, share your projects, and learn from other members of the community.

The forum is moderated by experienced Arduino users who are always ready to help.

3. Arduino Playground

Arduino Playground is a wiki-style website that contains a wealth of information on Arduino. It includes tutorials, example projects, and helpful tips and tricks. The site is user-driven, which means anyone can contribute to it. You can also find a list of recommended books and other resources on the site.

4. Adafruit Industries

Adafruit is a company that makes and sells electronics components and kits, including Arduino boards. They also have a vast library of tutorials and guides on their website, which are aimed at beginners and advanced users alike. Adafruit also offers excellent customer support, so if you have any questions, they are happy to help.

5. YouTube

YouTube is an excellent resource for learning Arduino. There are numerous channels dedicated to Arduino tutorials, such as Adafruit, Circuitoio, hecaworldunltd, and hecanet. You can also watch videos of other users' projects to get inspiration for your own.

In conclusion, these are just some of the recommended resources for beginners who want to learn Arduino. As you progress, you will discover more resources that suit your needs. Remember to keep learning and experimenting, and do not be afraid to ask for help along the way.

Commonly Used Components

In this section, we will discuss some of the most commonly used components in Arduino projects. These components are essential for building any electronic circuit and are used to perform various functions such as controlling voltage, current, and signal flow.

Resistors

Resistors are one of the essential components used in electronics. They are used to limit the current flow in a circuit, and their resistance is measured in ohms. The most commonly used resistors are carbon film resistors, metal film resistors, and wire wound resistors.

Capacitors

Capacitors are used to store electric charge and are used in various applications such as filtering, timing, and voltage regulation. They are available in different types such as ceramic capacitors, electrolytic capacitors, and tantalum capacitors.

Diodes

Diodes are used to control the flow of current in a circuit. They allow current to flow in only one direction, and their primary function is to convert AC to DC. The most commonly used diodes are rectifier diodes, Zener diodes, and light-emitting diodes (LEDs).

Transistors

Transistors are used to amplify or switch electronic signals. They are available in different types such as bipolar junction transistors (BJTs) and field-effect transistors (FETs). They are used in various applications such as amplifiers, oscillators, and switches.

LEDs

LEDs are used to indicate the status of a circuit or to provide lighting. They are available in different colors and are used in various applications such as traffic lights, displays, and indicators.

Sensors

Sensors are used to detect and measure physical quantities such as temperature, pressure, and light. They are essential components in various applications such as robotics, automation, and monitoring systems.

Conclusion

In summary, these are some of the most commonly used components in Arduino projects. These components are essential for building any electronic circuit and are used to perform various functions such as controlling voltage, current, and signal flow. As you start working on Arduino projects, you will come across many other components and learn how to use them effectively.

Sample Code

The best way to learn Arduino is by getting your hands 'dirty' and actually writing some codes. In this chapter, we will look at some sample code that will help you get started with Arduino programming.

Before we dive into the code, let us review the basics of Arduino programming. Arduino uses a simplified version of C++, which is a programming language used by many other microcontrollers. The code is written in an Integrated Development Environment (IDE), which is a software that allows you to write and upload code to the Arduino board.

You may also wish to run some project simulations from the https://www.circuito.io/ website to get a feel of the cool things that you can do with Arduinos at any time or ever before purchasing your first hardware.

Now, let us look at some sample code. The first program we will look at is the "Blink" program. This program will make an LED connected to pin 13 on the board blink on and off. Here is the code:

```
********************************
void setup() {
  pinMode(13, OUTPUT); // Set pin 13 as an output
}

void loop() {
  digitalWrite(13, HIGH); // Turn the LED on
  delay(1000); // Wait for 1 second
  digitalWrite(13, LOW); // Turn the LED off
  delay(1000); // Wait for 1 second
}
********************************
```

The "**setup**" function is called once when the board is powered up or reset. In this function, we set pin 13 as an output. The "loop" function is then called repeatedly as long as the board is powered up. In this function, we turn the LED on, wait for 1 second, turn the LED off, and wait for 1 second.

Another program we will look at is the "Button" program. This program will turn an LED on and off when a button connected to pin 2 is pressed. Here is the code:

```
********************************
int buttonPin = 2;      // Connect the button to pin 2
int ledPin = 13;        // Connect an LED to pin 13
```

```
int buttonState = 0;    // Keep track of the button state

void setup() {
  pinMode(buttonPin, INPUT);   // Set pin 2 as an input
  pinMode(ledPin, OUTPUT);     // Set pin 13 as an output
}

void loop() {
  buttonState = digitalRead(buttonPin);   // Read the button state
  if (buttonState == HIGH) {              // If the button is pressed
    digitalWrite(ledPin, HIGH);           // Turn the LED on
  } else {                                // If the button is not pressed
    digitalWrite(ledPin, LOW);            // Turn the LED off
  }
}
```
****

In this program, we define three variables: "buttonPin" for the pin connected to the button, "ledPin" for the pin connected to the LED, and "buttonState" to keep track of the button state. In the "setup" function, we set pin 2 as an input and pin 13 as an output. In the "loop" function, we read the button state and turn the LED on or off depending on the button state.

These are just two simple examples of Arduino programs. As you continue to learn and experiment with Arduino, you will find that the possibilities are endless. Start by modifying these sample programs and see what happens. Happy coding!

Troubleshooting Tips

Arduino is an amazing platform that has made it possible for anyone to experiment with electronics, regardless of their level of experience or expertise. However, just like any other technology, it is not immune to problems and glitches. In this subchapter, we will explore some tips and tricks that can help you troubleshoot common problems that you may encounter while using Arduino.

1.Check Your Connections

One of the most common causes of problems with Arduino is faulty or loose connections. Before you start troubleshooting any other issue, it is important to check all your connections carefully. Make sure that all wires and components are properly connected and firmly in place. If you find any loose connections, reconnect them and try again.

2. Verify Your Code

Another common cause of problems with Arduino is errors in your code. If you are having trouble getting your project to work, it is a good practice to double-check your code. Make sure that it is correctly written and that there are no syntax errors or other mistakes. You can use the Serial Monitor to print out debug messages and see what is going on behind the scenes.

3. Use the Built-In LED

If you are having trouble getting your project to work, you can use the built-in LED on your Arduino board to test whether it is functioning correctly. You can do this by uploading a simple sketch that turns the LED on and off. If the LED blinks, you know that your board is working properly.

4. Check Your Power Supply

Another common cause of problems with Arduino is a faulty power supply. Make sure that you are using the correct power supply for your board and that it is providing the correct voltage. If you are using a battery, make sure that it is fully charged.

5. Try a Different Board

If you have tried all of the above troubleshooting tips and are still having problems with your Arduino project, it may be time to try a different board. Sometimes boards can be faulty or damaged, and there is nothing you can do to fix them. Trying a different board can help you determine if the problem is with your code or your hardware.

In conclusion, Arduino is a fantastic platform for beginners to learn about electronics and programming. However, just like any other technology, it can sometimes have problems and glitches. But do not worry! We have some tips to help you troubleshoot and fix common issues you might encounter while working with Arduino.

Arduino is designed to be user-friendly, making it a great starting point for people who are new to electronics and coding. However, because it involves both hardware and software, things can sometimes go wrong. But with a little knowledge and a step-by-step approach, you can easily figure out and solve the most common problems.

First, familiarize yourself with the error codes and messages that Arduino might show you. These can give you clues about what is causing the issue. Next, make sure all your connections are secure and your power supply is working properly. Sometimes, loose wires or faulty connections can cause problems.

If you are writing code for Arduino and it is not working as expected, there are tools and libraries available that can help you find and fix mistakes in your code. Finally, do not forget to seek help from the Arduino community! There are many forums and online communities where you can ask questions and get support from experienced Arduino users.

In summary, Arduino is a great learning tool, but it can have its challenges. By following these troubleshooting tips, you will be able to tackle common problems and become more confident in your Arduino projects.

Common components for Arduino Projects

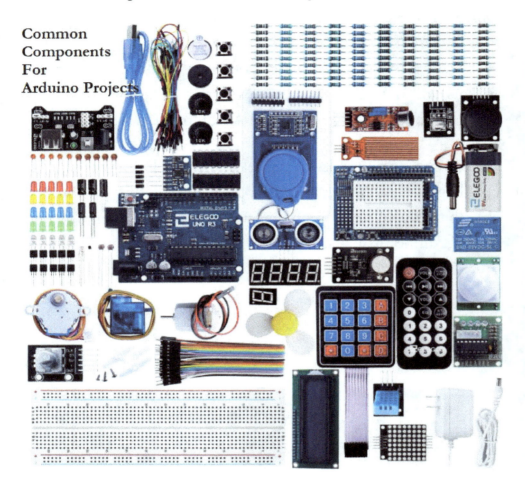